The Anxiety Workbook
With
Yoga Secrets

KEN HEPTIG

Ken Heptig

ISBN-13: 978-1548188351

ISBN-10: 1548188352

For information, submit a request: Goalyoga.com/connect

For bulk rate discounts visit: http://goalyoga.com/book-bundles/

Publisher: IT CIRCUS LLC

Charlotte, NC USA

Cover design by Anna Thompson

The author of this book does not dispense medical advice or prescribe any technique as a form of treatment for any physical, emotional, or medical problems without the advice of a physician, directly or indirectly. Readers should consult their own doctors or other qualified health professionals regarding the treatment of any medical conditions. No liability is assumed for losses or damages due to the information provided. You are responsible for your own choices, actions, and results.

ALSO BY KEN HEPTIG

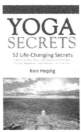

Yoga Secrets: 52 Life-Changing Secrets
Calm Your Pain, Stress, and Anxiety and Find More
Energy, Happiness, and Meaning in Your Life.

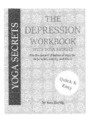

The Depression Workbook With Yoga Secrets
Use the Ancient Wisdom of Yoga for Relief
From Depression and Anxiety.

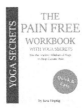

Spring 2018
The Pain Free Workbook With Yoga Secrets
Use the Ancient Wisdom of Yoga
to Live Pain Free and Enjoy Your Life.

Contents

1 ANXIETY

A panic attack can go from 0 to 100 in an instant.

Goal: Calm Your Anxiety Forever

One of my students purchased a 400-page workbook to help combat anxiety. If I had to work through that many pages, it would cause my anxiety to have anxiety! In fact, I might just decide it would be better to do nothing and just live with my problem. Worse yet, such methods often have a high-failure rate, and even those 400 pages might not prove fruitful in the end.

I was sure there had to be a better way, and after practicing yoga for two decades, I was convinced I would find a solution there. I have spent over ten years weaving the ancient wisdom of yoga into my classes. This required me to discover and refine the secrets until they were quick and easy, and I tested them time and time again, to see what works and what does not.

This Anxiety Workbook uses these yoga secrets, simplified for easy learning and understanding. The classes I offered varied from advanced power to relaxing, restorative yoga. At first, it was very awkward to teach the secrets. It did not seem to work, and I could find no books or articles to help. What my physical yoga practice taught me, however, is that we can become better at most things with practice. I refined and refined, until those secrets were simple and clear. Then one day, I realized I was connecting my students' physical world with their spiritual experience.

The ancient wisdom of yoga has gifted us with amazing insight into the workings of the human mind and body. One of these is clarity. In ancient times, Tibetan monks discovered that when things get messy in life, you need a clear mind to find your way. The problem is that when life gets messy, your mind also tends to get confused and messy. For the monks, the solution was to practice clearing the mind even when life was not messy. They called this new method meditation. The richest part of yoga is the spiritual and it requires practice. Tibetan monks still use the single word clear-seeing.

Understanding Anxiety

Anxiety often occurs with accompanying depression, so often that many consider them twin faces of the same disorder. Like depression, anxiety occurs in twice as many women as men.

Anxiety disorders comprise a group of related conditions, and anxiety can look very different from one person to the next. All anxiety disorders share persistent or severe fear or worry, even in circumstances when most people would not feel threatened.

Six Major Types of Anxiety Disorders
- Generalized anxiety disorder
- Panic disorder
- Obsessive-compulsive disorder
- Phobia
- Social anxiety disorder
- Post-traumatic stress disorder

When discussing anxiety, it is typical to hear about fear, worry, and panic, but we can really divide anxiety into four levels. While anxiety and fear begin in different parts of the brain, they do end up in the same place. To determine what level of anxiety a patient is suffering, they describe and rank their feelings and emotions. This is always subjective and open to interpretation.

Higher Risk Factors for Anxiety Disorders

- Being female
- Limited economic resources
- Being divorced or widowed
- Stressful events in childhood and adulthood
- Shyness as a child, being timid or negative
- Genetics

Anxiety Severity Scale

As mentioned, anxiety does entail various levels of severity, as the scale below indicates. Worry and mild concern can become anxiety. It can then move to fear, panic attacks, or even more severe consequences.

1. **Worry**   **Less severe**
2. **Anxiety**   ↓
3. **Fear**   ↓
4. **Panic**   **More severe**

Worry

Worry is the fear or concern that something bad might happen or that it has already happened. It can be useful when it spurs you to action and solves problems. The problem occurs when you become obsessed with what-ifs and worst-case scenarios. Life does not always make sense, or is it always fair, pleasant, or enjoyable. Life itself, feelings, and emotions can get messy, and when this happens, only a clear mind will help you find your way out of that mess.

Worry can become paralyzing and drain your energy, your *prana*, as known in Yoga, also known as your life force. The good news is that chronic worrying is a habit and a belief, so it can be changed. You can use yoga techniques to slow the activity in your mind, calm your emotions, and change how you see the world.

Anxiety

Anxiety is a natural response to stress or danger. It can result in nervousness, unease, or worried thoughts that something could go wrong or already has. It is perfectly normal to feel anxious when facing a challenging situation, and anxiety itself is not always a bad thing. It can keep you alert and improve your focus, as well as motivate you to solve problems and take action.

Anxiety becomes a disorder when it constantly or overwhelming disrupts your work, relationships, and daily activities. Anxiety disorders can prevent you from living the life you want to live.

Ten Differences Between Worry and Anxiety

Worry	Anxiety
In the head	In the body
Mild emotional distress	Severe emotional distress
More controllable	Less controllable
More realistic concerns	Less realistic concerns
Normal	Abnormal
Small impact on work or social life	Big impact on work or social life
Specific cause	Seemingly no specific cause
Temporary	Lingering or chronic
Triggers problem-solving	Paralyzes problem-solving
Verbal thoughts	Verbal thoughts and mental imagery

Fear

Fear is an emotion caused by the belief that something or someone is dangerous and may cause pain, damage, or discomfort. Without fear , we would not strive to protect ourselves from dangerous threats. We often react mistakenly with fear to many situations that pose no threat to our safety.

Panic

Panic is a sudden, overwhelming sensation of fear that produces hysterical or irrational behavior. Panic is so strong that it dominates all reasoning and logical thinking. It creates a frantic agitation, perhaps caused by our primitive fight-or-flight reaction. It can occur with or without cause, in individuals as well as large groups.

Panic Attack

Panic attack is a sudden feeling of terror that strikes without warning. These attacks can occur any time, without warning, including while sleeping. People who suffer from panic attacks may mistakenly believe they are having heart attacks or cardiac issues, because they manifest with physical symptoms. A panic attack occurs when fear and terror are out of proportion to what is really happening.

Depression

Depression is a mood disorder characterized by a persistent feeling of sadness and a loss of interest. Depression occurs when you feel worry, nervousness, or unease about an event or an uncertain outcome, and it affects how you feel, behave, and think. If you are depressed, you may find it difficult to fulfill responsibilities and participate in daily activities. It may leave you feeling useless and that your life is not worth living.

Stress

Stress is a state of mental or emotional strain from demanding circumstances. When you sense real or imagined danger, you invoke a fight-or-flight reaction, causing stress on your mind and body.

Symptoms of Anxiety

The lack of unnecessary struggle is freedom.

There are over 100 symptoms of anxiety, and some of the most common are:
- Backache
- Easily tiring
- Quick to be startled
- Churning stomach
- Diarrhea
- Frequent urination
- Headache
- Heart palpitations
- Increased heart rate
- Irritability
- Muscle tension
- Nausea
- Numbness or pins-and-needles feeling in arms, hands, or legs
- Rapid breathing
- Restlessness
- Sweating or flushing
- Trembling
- Trouble concentrating
- Difficulty falling or staying asleep

2 MENTAL HEALTH

Many people seem to use mental health and mental illness interchangeably, but while these are related, they represent different emotional states. *Mental health* is an emotional state of wellbeing, and it involves your ability to cope with the normal, everyday stresses of life. *Mental illness*, on the other hand, includes all diagnosable mental disorders or health conditions that involve alterations in thinking, mood, and behavior.

Your mental health includes your emotional, social, and psychological well-being. A mentally healthy person is capable of being a contributing member of society. It affects how you feel, think, and behave, and it determines how you handle stress and relationships. Your mental health will also have a great impact on the decisions you make, and studies show that positive mental health improves overall mental health.

Factors That Contribute to Mental Health
- Biological (brain chemistry)
- Family history
- Life experiences (trauma, abuse, etc.)

Ways to Calm Mental Health Issues
- Connect with others
- Get enough sleep
- Help others
- Learn coping techniques
- Physical exercise
- Positive attitude

Warning Signs of Mental Health
- Arguing frequently with family and friends
- Avoiding people and usual activities
- Changes in appetite and weight
- Feeling helpless, hopeless, or numb
- Feeling confused, angry, worried, forgetful, or scared
- Hearing voices or believing things that are not true
- Inability to handle daily tasks and duties at work or school
- Increase in drinking, smoking, or drug abuse
- Lack of energy
- Obsessive thoughts and memories
- Severe mood swings
- Sleeping too much or too little
- Thinking of harming yourself or others

Cognitive Distortions

"The primary cause of unhappiness is never the situation but your thoughts about it."

— Eckhart Tolle

Cognitive distortions are distorted or biased perceptions about yourself and the world around you. These thinking patterns can reinforce negative thoughts and bolster the effects of mental disorders, especially in anxiety and depression.

This biased way of thinking can interfere with the way you perceive events. The way you feel affects how you think, so cognitive distortions can lead to advanced negativity, leaving you with a pessimistic outlook toward people, events, and the world at large.

Cognitive Distortions that Can Increase Anxiety, Worry, and Stress

- All-or-nothing thinking — Seeing things in black-or-white, with no middle ground
- Always being right — Always trying to prove that your opinions/actions are correct
- Blaming — Holding other people responsible for your pain
- Expecting bad outcomes — Expecting the worst
- Control fallacies — Feeling controlled
- Diminishing the positive — Believing no positive events occur or matter
- Emotional reasoning — Believing that the way you feel reflects reality
- Fallacy of change — Expecting that other people will change to suit you
- Fallacy of fairness — Feeling resentful because you think you know what is fair
- Filtering — Focusing on the negatives and filtering out all the positives
- Heaven's reward fallacy — Expecting sacrifice and self-denial to pay off in the afterlife
- Jumping to conclusions — Creating negative interpretations without evidence
- Labeling — Beliefs based on mistakes and shortcomings
- Overgeneralization — Basing things on only one negative experiences
- Hypersensitive — Taking things personally and always feeling attacked/offended
- Strict limits — Strict beliefs about what you should and should not do

3 WORKBOOK GOALS

- Calm your anxiety forever.
- Learn and practice specific techniques to help.
- Breathing techniques to calm your emotions and slow the chaos in your mind.
- Turn negative self-talk into positive self-talk that will create a powerful force in your life.
- Identify bad habits and shift them to good ones.
- Find and manage specific triggers that increase your anxiety.

Simplicity and Clarity

Yoga has taught me to strive for clarity in everything I do. Therefore, this *Anxiety Workbook* embraces quick and easy methods, based on that simplicity.

Three Easy Steps

- Understand the concept.
- Learn the technique.
- Practice until it becomes a habit.

You may feel a bit of anxiety when you think about practicing the techniques you will learn, but my first word of advice is to relax and breathe. This is not a 400-page manual, nor will you need to practice forever. Sooner than you think, these helpful techniques will become habits and will feel like nothing more than a subconscious reaction.

In our effort to understand our world, we naturally break things down into smaller pieces. When we strive for simplicity and clarity, the world becomes easier to handle. Your mind will understand better when you organize and create levels, but if you strive too much to create greater levels of clarity, you will only increase specificity and lose simplicity. Remember that there is one simple goal: to calm your anxiety forever.

Most of us experience stress and anxiety, but many do not know the difference. Stress is a normal response to any threatening situation, while anxiety is your reaction to the stress often caused by worry.

Many of us find it hard to make changes that stick, but permanent changes are often the result of people stopping the process too soon. People also fail when they do not practice using what they have learned in their daily lives.

This workbook will help you practice three ways to inspire change and find freedom from anxiety. Each exercise provides an introduction, benefits, techniques, and practice. Learn these tools and apply them to your daily life and routines, and you will see positive results.

Change requires constant attention and effort. As you continue to practice the techniques, take note of the progress you make toward your goals.

Simple Works

> "Simplicity is the ultimate sophistication."
>
> — Leonardo da Vinci

Two Mental Obstacles to Simple Solutions

1. **I am not wrong.**
   Most of us hate being wrong, and finding out that we missed on something simple injures the ego, making us feel stupid or foolish or even inferior.

2. **My belief system is not wrong.**
   Simplicity challenges your belief system, the beliefs of your tribe. Sometimes it can present a challenge to your career or job. It may invalidate what you truly believe and all that you have been working toward in your adult life. These are very strong reasons for you to reject simple solutions, and they are the reasons many refuse to change belief systems.

Belief:	Hard work	= Better results	= Better solutions
Misbelief:	Simple solutions	= Less work	= Worse solutions
Misbelief:	Complex solutions	= More work	= Better solutions
Truth:	Simple solutions often	= More work	= Better solutions

Remember that your goal is to calm our anxiety forever and notice the end of the next two paths.

Path 1 – More and More Clarity Forever

Reading, understanding, and practicing through a 400-page book to eliminate anxiety could create ever more clarity and sophistication. With such an intricate guide, you will spend time obsessing and focusing on different levels of anxiety, comparing and contrasting countless theories about the problem. You will spend copious amounts of time reinforcing that you have a problem with anxiety. You invest even more time, work, and emotions in that problem, and you might be convinced that anxiety is actually a bigger, more dominant part of your life than you thought. Isn't this what you are trying to avoid? Surely, you do not want to be chained to weekly one-on-one office visits for the rest of your life.

Path 2 – More Simplicity, Mindfulness, and Enjoy Life

The path of more simplicity minimizes the time you will waste reinforcing your anxiety, rendering it a smaller, more manageable part of our life. It will free up more time for you, so you can be released from anxiety and enjoy your life without so much worry and fear to hold you down.

4 YOGA

Starting Your Physical Yoga Practice (Optional)

While it is optional, I strongly recommend that you begin to participate in physical yoga practice. This will quicken and deepen your personal lifetime transformation.

At least try several beginner classes. In these classes, you will learn the names of poses, alignment, and the proper use of blocks and straps. It will also increase your comfort and confidence and better prepare you for your first non-beginner class. A good yoga foundation increases your chances of making yoga an ongoing practice.

When you start your yoga journey, keep an open heart and mind. Do not give up on class too soon. Listen to your teacher to learn the poses and alignment. It is fine to look at others for guidance, but do not compare yourself to your classmates or be too judgmental with yourself. Yoga is not about competition! Just work on enjoying your practice.

Before Starting
- Consider a beginner class or decide what level you can handle.
- Be honest about your current level of fitness.
- Shop around for prices and special deals for new students.
- If you have any health condition, talk with your doctor before starting.

Finding Yoga Classes
- Check with local yoga studios, the YMCA, and fitness clubs and gyms.
- Search online for free, inexpensive, trial, or donation classes.
- Investigate one- or five-class passes and avoid being talked into a long-term contract.
- Try several different places and teachers.

Other Options
- Buy a DVD.
- Search for online yoga instructional.
- Consider private yoga lessons.
- Look for yoga classes on television or streaming services and fitness channels.

Other Things to Do
- Get to know your classmates.
- Learn to use blocks and a strap; these are not just for beginners.
- Remain in class for the full duration.

Things You Should Know
- Be kind to your body and yourself.
- Keep an open heart and mind about your experience.
- Let go of attachments before you practice.
- Know that no one is staring at you; your classmates are focused on their own alignment, poses, and the deepening of their practice.

Physical Benefits of Yoga

Improves
- All-round fitness
- Athletic performance
- Balance
- Breathing
- Cardiovascular and circulatory health
- Cartilage and joint strength
- Flexibility
- Immune system functionality
- Posture
- Respiration and vitality
- Sleep

Increases
- Blood flow
- Bone strength
- Energy
- Heart rate
- Muscle strength

Decreases
- Blood pressure
- Blood sugar
- Digestive problems
- Muscle tension
- Allergies and viruses
- Spine problems

Other
- Maintains nervous system
- Regulates adrenal glands
- Relaxes
- Supports connective tissue
- Uses sounds to soothe sinuses

Emotional Benefits of Yoga

Improves
- Ability to stay drug free
- Awareness of the present moment
- Awareness of transformation
- Calmness
- Concentration
- Happiness
- Healing in the mind's eye
- Healthy lifestyle
- Inner peace
- Intuition
- Memory
- Mind-body connection
- Mood
- Positive outlook
- Relationships
- Self-acceptance
- Self-control
- Self-esteem
- Social skills

Decreases
- Anxiety
- Depression
- Hostility
- Pain
- Stress

5 THE ANCIENT WISDOM
Yoga Secrets

The longest journey is the journey inward.

Yoga does not focus on your goal or destination. Instead, it aims to help you on your journey through life. Yoga is a method by which you can avoid and manage threats and obstacles. When you follow the proper methods, you can lower anxiety and flow through life with ease.

Yoga often refers to the non-physical philosophy or spiritual side. This part of yoga can help you handle thoughts and sensations when events occur that elicit a response. It can help you stay mindful and overcome obstacles and challenges. You can learn specific yoga techniques to help manage your thoughts, sensations, threats, obstacles, and challenges during your journey.

Yoga secrets is an easy way to learn and enjoy the ancient wisdom of yoga, as discussed previously in my *Yoga Secrets: 52 Life-Changing Secrets,* a book that follows the same path as the ancient wisdom found in *The Yoga Sutras: Eight Limbs of Yoga* by Patanjali. This ancient wisdom is about 2,000 years old and offers guidance on how to live a meaningful, purposeful life.

Placebo Phrases

When I started my yoga practice, I heard teachers repeating phrases like, "Be mindful," "Set an intention," and, "Stay present," but rarely did they explain the meaning of these. When they did offer explanations, these were vague and confusing, especially for a beginner like me. Although my human senses could not detect what was happening, my mind still created an explanation that was wrong. I believed the students with the big smiles were telling the world they truly understood and had found enlightenment. I practice what I learn, and joy and happiness were among the concepts in yoga. My happiness for my fellow students who had found enlightenment was sincere, but I did not find that enlightenment for myself.

In time, I became more confused, and that contributed to greater anxiety. I wondered why I was still so lost when my classmates seemed to easily understand. I knew it was time to put my ego aside and ask the allegedly enlightened students to explain the meaning of the phrases used in class. They responded with silence and confusion of their own, until someone admitted, "Well, uh…you know, I'm not really sure what they mean."

In the end, I realized that those phrases were simply ploys to generate good feelings and entice students back to class. With that in mind, I began to refer to these as *placebo phrases*, empty words used to lure people end. After that, I found it easier to simply smile in class, since I understood the intention of the phrase.

The placebo phrases seemed to become emptier and more meaningless as time went on, and my confusion and anxiety increased. Only after my own extensive research and reading did I feel I understood the meaning of many of the life-changing secrets of yoga. My next step increased my anxiety even more, when I tried making the yoga secrets quick and easy, so I could teach them to my own students without confusing them. That required constant testing and refining for over a decade, through thousands of yoga classes. Yoga teaches us to seek the truth in life, and this may mean questioning and changing our beliefs as we seek that truth.

The Yoga Sutras of Patanjali

"Mastery of yoga is really measured by how it influences our day-to-day living, how it enhances our relationships, how it promotes clarity and peace of mind."

—T.K.V. Desikachar

The Yoga Sutras of Patanjali, created sometime between 100 to 300 BCE, resulted in yoga practice long before the text was printed. "The Eight Limbs of Yoga" is the second chapter in that work by Patanjali, the author or compiler whom many know as the father of yoga. It is possible, however, that the text was provided through a group effort that spanned several generations.

Around 3,500 years ago, yoga was a spiritual, meditative practice, not physical, with postures. Hatha Yoga changed this in the tenth century and included physical postures, pranayama breath control, and spiritual intention. Yogis found it difficult to sit for long periods of time during meditation as they tried to connect with the spiritual world. Physical yoga poses made it easier to meditate, focus, and move into stillness. Thus, the physical practice of yoga became a portal to the spiritual world. To study yoga in ancient times, students lived with their teachers, but that is difficult to even imagine in modern times.

The Eight Limbs of Yoga is a systematic method of levels like those referenced in the anxiety severity scale offered earlier. A yogi moves sequentially through the levels from limb one to limb eight. Notice that only one of the eight limbs is about *asana*, the physical practice of yoga.

The last, or eighth, limb is *Samadhi*, which means enlightenment or union with the divine. During your journey through The Eight Limbs, you will remove your identity and obstacles. As you practice the first two, *yamas* and *niyamas*, you work through a process called attainment, fruits, or acquisition. Attainment uncovers things that already exist. The first five rungs, or limbs, sharpen your razor, your attention for discrimination. You can then use this sharpened razor during the last three limbs of concentration, meditation, and Samadhi to peel away your layers of habit and misbelief and find your true self.

Limb 8: Samadhi (Enlightenment)

The eighth, or final, limb of yoga is Samadhi. The first seven limbs are worked through in order before you get to this stage, which Patanjali describes as transcendence of the self through meditation. You move beyond time, form, and space. Samadhi is the ultimate stage in yoga, in which you will find a supreme consciousness.

In the early state of Samadhi, you lose self-consciousness, or your sense of I. The process of meditation and the object of meditation become one.

Samadhi involves a series of states and experiences. *The Yoga Sutras of Patanjali* describes various types of Samadhi that you must pass through on your way to enlightenment. The name of the highest stage of illumination is *dharma megha Samadhi*, which liberates you from all limitations of body and mind. During Samadhi, you achieve discriminative enlightenment, where you use *viveka*, razor-like attention to divide the seer and the seen.

The Eight Limbs of Yoga

Limb No.	Name	Description
	Yama	Universal morality (values)
2	Niyama	Personal observances (laws)
3	Asanas	Body postures
4	Pranayama	Breathing, control of pranas
5	Pratyahara	Control of the senses
6	Dharana	Concentration, perception, awareness
7	Dhyana	Devotion, meditation on the divine, keenly aware without focus
8	Samadhi	Union with the divine

Limb 1: Yama (Universal Morality, Values)

The first limb is the *yamas*, moral constraints to focus on how you behave and conduct yourself in life. These guide you to restrain behaviors spawned by grasping, aversion, hatred, and delusion. Yamas suggest avoiding violence, lying, stealing, greed, and wasting energy.

The Five Yamas	
Ahimsa	nonviolence, kindness
Satya	truthfulness
Asteya	non-stealing
Brahmacharya	moderation, continence
Aparigraha	generosity, non-covetousness

Limb 2: Niyama (Personal Observances, Laws)

The five *niyamas* refer to self-discipline and spiritual practices. They include your wellbeing, as well as the wellbeing of others. While they do not determine right from wrong, the niyamas are rules for you to follow. They do not mention heaven or hell; rather, they suggest that you avoid behaviors that produce suffering and instead embrace those that lead to happiness. Niyamas let you create harmony within you and with your external world, without telling you what to do, because what you do is for you to decide.

Benefits occur when you remove identity and obstacles. Patanjali describes this process as attainment, fruits, or acquisition. This attainment comes from uncovering what is already there.

The Five Niyamas	
Saucha	cleanliness, purity
Samtosa	contentment
Tapas	heat; spiritual austerities
Svadhyaya	study of the scriptures and oneself
Isvara Pranidhana	surrender to God

6 NON-REACTION: THE POWER TO CHANGE AN EVENT

If you cannot control your thoughts, the world will control them for you.

Your mind has evolved to seek the negative. During evolution, we faced many predators and obstacles that could easily end our life, resulting in a strong fight-or-flight reflex. Many of those predators and obstacles are no longer a threat to our survival, yet we still treat minor threats as if they are. This can increase your heart rate and cause irregular or labored breathing, as well as other symptoms.

The good news is that you can learn to keep minor events from triggering your fight-or-flight reflex. When an event elicits a response, you can practice non-reaction, just pausing and refusing to respond. This gives you time to decide how to react, especially since the need to react to an argument or perceived obligation is often insignificant or based on your own misbelief.

With non-reaction, you discover that you are not your thoughts and sensations. Rather, you are that space between thought and sensations, what yoga refers to as your *true self*.

A subtle difference exists between awareness of a thought and thinking a thought. *Awareness* of a thought is a texture or a light, distant feeling. *Thinking* a thought elicits tension in your body, such as muscle contraction, an increase in heart rate, or irregular breathing.

One way to practice non-reaction is to become an observer and take notice of your thoughts. When you pause and do not react to an event, it gives you time to catch and examine your thoughts. That quiet time between thoughts and sensations allows you to observe your thoughts and notice your habits. Practicing non-reaction creates a pause in your actions and emotions, so you can decide if and how you will react. It helps keep your emotions, habits, and misbelief from deciding for you. In essence, non-reaction keeps the world from controlling your life.

Watching your thoughts is like watching the clouds come and go as they float through the sky. You may notice the clouds, but you do not attach yourself to them; you only observe them as they come and go. Similarly, when you practice non-reaction, you observe without instantly reacting. Non-reaction helps you find freedom from the world that tries to control you through your emotions.

Non-reaction also enables you to change your thoughts and improve your life. It takes practice and mindfulness to stay in the present, in the moment. When you slow your thoughts and sensations, you can better combat stress and anxiety and improve concentration, clarity, happiness, and freedom. Practice can make this easier, until it feels more natural, like an automatic reflex.

Observing events allows you to act as a bystander. You will notice how your habits and misbelief control you in various circumstances. If you observe, you will see how to better live your life. When you stay in the present moment, you do not control your thoughts; you simply keep your thoughts, habits, and misbelief from controlling your life. Non-reaction provides you with an opportunity to calm your mind, concentrate, and move into stillness. It gives you a chance to notice and change your habits and misbelief.

Reaction to any event has the power to change that event. Find that space between your thoughts and sensations, your true self. When you find that quiet space, you will find stillness, and in stillness, you can find freedom from your anxiety.

7 MINDFULNESS

The only time that exists is the present moment.

The present moment is the only time when you have power and control. Fear pulls you back from the present moment, and desire pushes you past it. Both distract you from enjoying and living your life in the here and now.

Mindfulness is a practice that is thousands of years old. It requires you to stay active and pay attention, without judgment or attachment, to what is happening around you. You must carefully observe and accept your emotions, feelings, and thoughts. You stay in the present moment and thereby keep the world from passing you by. Mindfulness can calm your anxiety and assist you in acing your daily challenges. When you are in the present moment, it feels as if time ceases to exist, and it provides an escape from attachment to your problems.

To be mindful, you must purposefully observe what is happening around you. This creates clarity in your thoughts and in your life. Treat the present moment as your first choice, regardless of the circumstances. Experience and respond to things happening now. Stay present to cut back your anxiety. Mindfulness can help you find a new way of seeing things.

Practicing Mindfulness

To practice mindfulness, you must stop racing around and focus on what you are doing. Develop a habit of steady and calm breathing. This will slow your heart rate, calm your emotions, ease your mind, relax your muscles, and soften your body. Focus on inhaling and exhaling; inhale only as your exhaling comes to an end. Breathe out what you do not want and breathe in gratitude and happiness.

Many important events in your life occur when you are not in the present, and you miss out on more important events and opportunities than you realize. Do not live as if you are not here. Your life will become easier, and you will find more energy and create more happiness in your life. Living in the past or the future keeps you from living in the present. It causes you to go through life as if you have never really lived.

Most of us find it difficult to stay mindful and in the present. It is natural to worry about the future or spend too much time dwelling on the past, but there is a time and place for everything, including reflecting on past actions and planning for future success. The exercise allows you to focus on the present moment, the only time when you truly have power and control. Explore three areas that keep you from being mindful and practice activities to overcome these obstacles.

First, we will cover habits, learning to unlearn, and developing persistence. Your habits often cause you to live on autopilot and prevent you from living in the present moment. Learning to identify bad habits and replace them with good habits can help you find freedom from the world that aims to control you through your emotions. This can lower your anxiety and makes it easier to stay mindful and in the present moment. Creating positive habits, correcting misbeliefs, and letting go of things you cannot control will free up your prana, your life force, for more important things. Remember to accept where you are today. Make the easy changes first, and the harder ones will become easier. Always keep an open heart and mind.

Ways to Practice Mindfulness

Ask Better Questions
- Why are you here?
- What are your assumptions and beliefs, and why do you have them?
- What are your habits, and why do you have them?
- What are your thoughts, and why do you have them?

Attitude
- Be determined and follow your passion.
- Learn to focus.

Connect
- Connect with nature.
- Connect with the present moment.
- Connect with your senses.

Disconnect
- Put your phone in airplane mode when in meetings.
- Turn off your phone for several hours.

Gratitude
- Tell someone how much you appreciate them.
- Write a personal thank-you or love note.

Non-reaction
- Observe your thoughts without attachment.
- Observe your thoughts without reacting.
- Practice acceptance.
- Remain patient.

Nourish
- Drink water all day.
- Eat fresh, whole foods.
- Eat slowly and savor every bite.

Observe
- Observe your breathing.
- Observe your emotions.
- Observe your thoughts.

Practice

- Practice steady, calm breathing.
- Practice deep breathing.
- Practice mindfulness.
- Practice transformational listening.

Simplify

- Act slowly and deliberately.
- Do one thing at a time.
- Eliminate distractions.
- Eliminate the unimportant.
- Slow down.

Take Action

- Move around and stretch often.
- Take short mindfulness breaks
- Use reminders, written and visual.
- Write down your top three priorities every morning.

Benefits of Mindfulness

Lowers

- Anxiety
- Blood pressure
- Depression
- Heart rate

Healthier

- Mind and body
- Social life and relationships

Increased

- Awareness, attention, and focus
- Clarity in thinking and perception
- Feeling of calmness, stillness, and openness
- Feeling of gratitude
- Immune function
- Path to insight
- Resilient mind
- Spiritual growth

8 PHYSICAL EXERCISE

> If you only exercise when you feel good, how will you exercise often enough to feel good all the time?

Fitness means being able to do physical activity and having the energy to function at as high a level as possible. You can improve your health greatly by being just a little fitter than you are now. Start slowly and gradually, then increase your intensity. If you have any health condition, please talk to your doctor before beginning any physical exercise program.

It is important to avoid inactivity. Any amount of physical activity is better than inactivity and has health benefits.

The Center for Disease Control Minimum Recommendations for a Healthy Adult
- 2.5 hours per week of moderate-intensity aerobic physical activity like brisk walking or tennis or
- 1.25 hours per week of vigorous-intensity aerobic physical activity like jogging or swimming laps

Anything that is good for your heart is highly likely to also be great for your brain, and aerobic exercise are tremendous for both. Aerobics improves brain function and acts as a first aid kit for damaged brain cells. Physical activity can improve cognitive function, regardless of age.

Three-Legged Stool
Yoga believes everything is connected to everything else in the universe. To live a healthy life, you must have balance in your *yin* (passive) and *yang* (vigorous). The yin and yang complement one another, creating balance and harmony, and this balance is necessary for a healthy interrelationship between a clear mind, a strong body, and an enlightened spirit, like a three-legged stool.

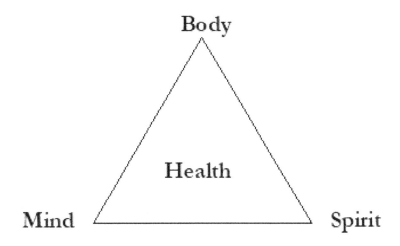

Benefits of Physical Exercise

Studies show that exercise is a very effective treatment for anxiety and depression, and it does not harbor any of the negative side effects of medication. When you maintain a regular exercise schedule, it can prevent you from relapsing into high anxiety. Exercising also has a remarkable effect on your productivity, an effect that is multiplied over your lifetime if you continue a daily regimen of physical activity. The benefits of exercise are truly enormous.

Exercise relieves stress and tension and boosts your physical and mental energy. It releases endorphins in your brain, the feel-good chemicals that encourage positive thinking, thus distracting you from negativity and anxiety.

Instant Benefits of Exercise

The moment you start to exercise, the benefits begin. Changes start in seconds with an increase in your heart rate and more blood pumping to your muscles. You will burn calories and receive an almost instant mood boost.

Increases

- Ability to control addiction
- Brainpower
- Capacity to function
- Chance of longevity
- Creativity
- Energy
- Endorphins (happy chemicals)
- Memory
- Mental health and mood
- Productivity
- Relaxation
- Self-confidence
- Sleeping comfort
- Strength of bones and muscles
- Weight control

Lowers

- Anxiety and depression
- Cardiovascular disease
- Cognitive decline
- Risk of certain cancers
- Stress
- Type 2 diabetes

9 TECHNIQUES AND EXERCISES

"Yoga provides us tools and techniques to lead a stress-free and a tension-free life."

—Sri Sri Ravi Shanka

A *technique* is a method of performing a task, and yoga relies on very specific techniques to perform a wide range of specific tasks. The ancient wisdom of yoga includes several breathing techniques, and we will cover three that will calm your anxiety.

Breathing
We will explore breath awareness, breathing to calm emotions, and Ujjayi Pranayama breathing. With proper technique, breathing can soothe the nervous system, calm the mind, relax the muscles, soften the body, slow down the heart rate, lower blood pressure, and calm anxiety.

We will practice breath awareness, breathing techniques, and breathing with a steady and calm breath.

Self-talk
Your message to yourself matters. Your body hears every thought you think and every word you speak. It reacts to everything you tell yourself. Clarity in your words creates clarity in your life.

We will use motor imagery, positive self-talk, positive thinking, clarity, and mantras to help us turn negative self-talk into positive self-talk.

Habit Shifting
Bad habits can keep you from accomplishing goals and fully living your life. Those who break bad habits often replace them with different ones. We will practice habit shifting from your old habit to your new habit, because bad habits waste your prana, your life force, which you need to focus more energy on the important things in life.

We will practice shifting a habit from bad to good, regardless of the habit you are trying to break. To shift that habit, we will use triggers, awareness, patterns, learning to unlearn, and not giving up too soon.

Exercises A-F
A: Breath Awareness
B: Ujjayi Pranayama Breathing Technique
C: Mantras for Calming Anxiety
D: Identify and Change Negative Self-Talk
E: Shift a Bad Habit, Part 1
F: Shift a Bad Habit, Part 2

10 BREATHING

Change how you breathe to change how you see.

You cannot live without anxiety or fear, but breathing techniques can help you manage them. This allows you to fully experience and enjoy life in the present moment. Other techniques help you manage things that cause anxiety. You can find freedom from habits, emotions, and lack of confidence. Before we begin, you must understand why so many of us find ourselves trapped in high anxiety.

The world controls you through your emotions, and your mind has evolved to seek the negative. Your fight-or-flight reflex increases your heart rate and causes breathing to become shallow and irregular, but you can learn to keep these minor events from triggering that reflex by using breathing to calm your emotions.

When a minor event tries to control you, try practicing non-reaction by pausing and not reacting. As we have discussed, this gives you time to decide how to react. This becomes easier with practice and by staying mindful.

Your habits, fight-or-flight reflexes, and even the way you speak to yourself can keep you trapped. *The Anxiety Workbook With Yoga Secrets* includes three techniques to help you learn how to break your habits. You can learn to control your emotions and reflexes using breathing techniques. This changes the way your subconscious views yourself. Practice can make you better at most things, so keep practicing these exercises until they become habits. The exercises will help you find freedom from our anxiety.

Yoga does not teach you to pretend that things are not happening around you or to lie to yourself. This would create confusion and an unhealthy life journey. Instead, yoga teaches you to seek the truth and manage what is happening around you so you can flow through life with ease.

Breathing in yoga is your Prana, your life force connection. Pranayama breathing is the control of your life force through your breath, involving the measuring, controlling, and directing of your breath. When you join the inhale with the exhale, you find perfect relaxation and balance in all your body activities and functions.

Proper breathing offers more oxygen to your mind and body. Pranayama breathing helps you enjoy more happiness, weight loss, energy, and a longer life. Yoga can teach you how to integrate your breathing, mind, and emotions. This can help you keep your emotions, thoughts, and habits from controlling your life. In yoga, you do not control your thoughts; you just keep them from controlling you.

When you slow down, pause, and observe, you will rise above the noise of your thoughts and sensations. This will give you quiet time to observe your thoughts and sensations. It helps you understand your habits and create a path toward personal transformation. When you pause before reacting, you find the freedom to become the person you wish to be rather than allowing your past habits to control your life.

Breathing to Calm Emotions

"It's not stress that kills us. It is our reaction to it."

—Hans Selye

The power and benefits of yoga breathing over the central nervous system has piqued the interest of scientists and doctors for years. We can divide our nervous system into two modes: sympathetic (fight or flight) and parasympathetic (rest and digest). The sympathetic fight-or-flight phenomenon developed as a survival mechanism in ancient times. The sympathetic activates the adrenal medulla gland, which then releases hormones into the bloodstream. These hormones cause the body to speed up, tense up, and become more alert. The parasympathetic system kicks in even when no immediate threat or danger is present. Long periods of relaxation let the body return to balance and recover as the immune and digestion systems take priority.

Although you become more alert when you activate your sympathetic nervous system, experts have found that this takes a huge toll on your body. It evolved as a way to protect us from real physical harm like that imposed by dangerous animals or people. You can also trigger your sympathetic nervous system with other stressful situations like work deadlines, arguments, or too much anxiety.

At first, researchers believed we could not control this automatic switch between the systems, even when we are in no true physical danger. In the 1970s, Dr. Herbert Benson published *The Relaxation Response*, and in his book, he described the breathing techniques used by Eastern health practitioners and yogis for centuries. The book argues that one can trigger the parasympathetic nervous system to kick in and counter the fight-or-flight response to daily stresses by controlling one's breath. Since then, multiple studies have expanded upon and proven his theory that breathing techniques can override our automatic switch to the fight-or-flight mode.

You can learn to invoke the opposite reflex, the relaxation response. To do this, you need to use a proper breathing technique. Continuous practice of breathing for your relaxation response can help you change your fight-or-flight reflex and keep it from responding as often during your day. I find it amazing that it took until the 1970s for Western culture to recognize and claim, as their discovery, something yogis have known for thousands of years.

Learning breath-control techniques and staying mindful of your breath allows you to gain control over your respiratory system and your life. Be mindful of how your breath, mind, and emotions weave together. When breathing steadily and calmly, you lower your heart rate, slow brain activity, calm emotions, soften your body, and relax your muscles. You strengthen your respiratory system, soothe your nervous system, and lower your external cravings.

Breathing can make a healthy person sick or a sick person healthy. It cleanses the lungs, oxygenates the blood, and purifies your nerves. It calms the mind and clears out negative emotions. Your breathing reveals your inner feelings and emotions; it connects what you know with what you feel. Steady, calm breathing can ease physical pain, mental stress, depression, and anxiety. It can improve overall health and increase happiness. Exhale the bad; inhale the good.

Calming your desires and cravings gives you freedom from emotions, habits, and misbelief. Freedom from your emotions helps your mind move into stillness, leaving space for concentration.

Exercise A: Breath Awareness

> When you own your breath, nobody can steal your peace.

During this two-part breathing exercise, you will practice being aware of your natural breath. You will then learn and practice a basic breathing technique.

Breath Awareness

Using this breathing technique, you will focus your attention on one thing: your breath.

1. Sit or lie in a comfortable, quiet place. Relax and close your eyes. Place your left hand just below your navel and your right one over your heart. Breathe in and out in steady, calm breaths. All breathing is through your nose while keeping your lips sealed.

2. Learn to notice your breath as it flows in and out of your body. Do not try to control it in any way. Do not become anxious or feel you need to react. Simply observe your breath and sensations and know that you are neither of these. Rather, you are that space between thought and sensation, the space yoga calls your true self.

3. Change your posture and repeat the exercise for Body Position B.

	Body Position A	Body Position B
1 How do you feel as you inhale?		
2 What is happening in your body?		
3 Where do you feel your breath go?		
4 How do you feel at the crest of each inhale?		

	Body Position A	Body Position B
6 How do you feel when you exhale?		
7 Where does the point of exhalation start?		
8 Is the pace of your inhale different from the pace of your exhale?		
9 Do you notice changes in your body during the pause after your exhale?		
10 Are the pauses before and after your inhale different?		
11 Does your breathing feel comfortable or uncomfortable?		
12 Is your breath steady and calm?		

11 PRANAYAMA BREATHING

One type of pranayama breathing is Ujjayi. The translation for Ujjayi (pronounced *oo-jai*) is "victorious breath," but it is also known as the oceanic breath. Yogis have used Ujjayi breathing for thousands of years. You can improve how you feel by regulating the length, air volume, and sound of your inhales and exhales.

It is important to relax during Ujjayi breathing, which will naturally lengthen your breath. Too much effort can cause a grating sound. On the contrary, producing the pleasing ocean sound requires a delicate balance of effort, not too little and not too much.

All inhales and exhales are through your nose, with your lips sealed. This helps to create a resistance to air from your breath. Nostril breathing helps you support a steady, calm breath.

In addition to steady and calm, your breathing should be continuous, an uninterrupted cycle of inhales and exhales. To make the Ujjayi sound, seal your lips and inhale through your nose, slightly deeper than normal. Constrict the muscles in the back of your throat as you slowly exhale through your nose, as in whispering or breathing in and out through a thin straw. Inhaling with a gentle, calm breath and exhaling against this resistance creates a steady, soothing sound, like ocean waves rolling in and out.

The sound between inhales and exhales should remain consistent, and you can observe the quality of your Ujjayi breath by listening to its sound. Notice if your breathing feels strained, irregular, or forced.

Your breathing should feel energizing and relaxing. In the Yoga Sutra, Patanjali suggests that breath should be both *dirga* (long) and *suksma* (smooth).

You can use specific breathing rhythms and techniques to help your body, mind, and emotions.

Exercise B: Ujjayi Pranayama Breathing Technique

1. Sit in a comfortable position.
2. Close your eyes and place your right hand over your heart and your left just below your navel.
3. As you inhale, feel how your belly expands. Take several natural, deep inhales and exhales.
4. Inhale and exhale through your mouth, as if trying to fog up a mirror, making a "haaaah" sound. Noise is part of this technique.
5. Seal your lips and inhale through your nose, slightly deeper than normal. Exhale slowly through your nose while constricting the muscles in the back of your throat.
6. Try to create the same sound and sensation while inhaling and exhaling.
7. Have fun playing with your Ujjayi breathing by taking deeper breaths and pausing before exhaling.

Benefits of Pranayama Breathing

"Learn how to exhale. The inhale will take care of itself."

—Carla Melucci Ardito

Pranayama breathing can soothe the nervous system, calm the mind, relax the muscles, soften the body, slow the heart rate, lower blood pressure, and more.

When you focus on breathing, you can calm feelings of agitation. The fluctuations of your mind slows, allowing you to observe without constantly reacting to your emotions. You can calm your anxiety with the steady, calm, rhythmic nature of your pranayama breath.

You cannot have high anxiety or depression while undergoing Ujjayi breathing. It is about being able to change the way you feel by not letting your emotions control your life.

Calms
- Feelings of irritation and frustration
- The mind and body
- Feeling present and aware
- Instills endurance
- Relieves tension

Heat and Energy
- Builds energy
- Increases and regulates internal body heat
- Encourages the free flow of prana (life force)
- Instills endurance

Focus
- Diminishes distractions
- Improves concentration

Balances and Regulates
- Balances cardiovascular and respiratory systems
- Detoxifies the mind and body
- Maintains constant rhythm during yoga practice
- Increases oxygen in the blood
- Lessens headache pain
- Regulates blood pressure
- Relieves of sinus pressure
- Strengthens nervous and digestive systems

12 SELF-TALK

"The most important decision we make is whether we believe we live in a friendly or hostile universe."

—Albert Einstein

As Einstein suggested, if you automatically decide the universe is an unfriendly place, you will only create bigger walls to keep out the unfriendliness and isolate and/or destroy yourself in the process. If the universe is neither friendly nor unfriendly, then you are doomed to be a victim of a random toss of the dice, and your life has no real purpose or meaning. If you decide the universe is a friendly place, you will use technology and science to understand that universe. It really is a simple, logical principle: You get what you give.

If you suffer from chronic anxiety, you may see the world as a hostile universe or more dangerous than it actually is. You may think things will turn out poorly. You may treat negativity as if it is a fact. As mentioned earlier in this book, cognitive distortions are pessimistic, irrational attitudes that are not based on reality. These misbeliefs can become a habit that causes you to react instantly to your emotions.

We all hold internal conversations as we go about our daily lives. Psychologists refer to this as *self-talk*. You form opinions and evaluations, a play-by-play of what you are doing as you are doing it. When upbeat, self-validating self-talk occurs, the results can boost your productivity and self-esteem. Negative self-talk, on the other hand, can cripple your emotions. Saying nice things to yourself can boost your mood, but most people are unaware of the power of self-talk.

Neurologists have been exploring this concept for the past century. In 1911, Drs. Henry Head and Gordon Morgan Holmes published a series of papers about their study on the mind-body connection. In the study, they used a style that was popular at the time, the large hats with giant feathers at the top, worn by the fashionable women of the early twentieth century. Holmes and Head noticed that women who donned such headwear often ducked every time they walked through doors, whether they were wearing the hats at the time or not. As humorous as this was, the study concluded some important scientific considerations: The subject's mental self was wearing the hat, even if her physical self was not. In similar studies, patients with eating disorders turned to the side or tried to unnecessarily squeeze through spaces, even though they had plenty of room.

Although neuroscientists are still trying to understand how this works, it does reveal how much our internal view of ourselves affects how we function in the external world. You need a very specific sense of yourself if you are to understand how to move and function. This allows you to walk around without bumping into things or reach your hand out for that mug of coffee without just grasping at air.

Your message to yourself matters. You can change how you view reality by changing negative words to positive ones. For example, you can soften your words by saying, "I feel discomfort," rather than stating, "I am in pain." You can say, "I am curious," instead of, "I am angry." You become what you think. A clear, positive message creates clear, positive thoughts, and these can help you make better choices and enjoy a healthier, happier journey through life.

Motor Imagery

"All that we are is the result of what we have thought."

—Buddha

Motor imagery is the subject of much research by noteworthy neurologists. Findings on this internal sense of oneself shows that we use the same neurological networks to imagine movement and witness actual movement. When you practice visualizing or imagining movement, it can have the same effect on your brain as actually practicing it in the physical world. This can also lead to similar improvements in performance. Likewise, practicing positive thoughts and words can improve overall self-esteem, silence your inner critic, and improve the reality of the world in which you live.

Positive Thinking

"Watch your thoughts; they become words.

Watch your words; they become actions.

Watch your actions; they become habits.

Watch your habits; they become character.

Watch your character; for it becomes your destiny."

—Upanishads, 800 to 500 BCE

Positive thinking does not mean you must ignore uncomfortable or painful situations or pretend they do not exist. Again, your body listens to every thought you think and every word you speak. Positive thinking means you approach uncomfortable situations in a more positive, more productive way. You stay mindful and know that you can manage these unpleasant situations. When you practice optimistic thinking, the best will happen, not the worst.

Positive thinking often starts with self-talk. Self-talk is the continuous stream of unspoken thoughts that run through your head. These can be positive or negative. Some self-talk comes from a place of logic and reason, while some comes from habits or misbeliefs you get from others or misguided explanations you have created in your own mind.

If you allow negative self-talk, your outlook toward the universe will be more pessimistic, and you will be more likely to keep others out of your life. If your self-talk is positive, you are more optimistic, more open to the world, and you practice positive thinking. Research suggests that positive self-talk creates positive thinking, optimism, and a richer feeling of happiness.

A clear, positive attitude helps you create clear, positive thoughts. Use positive thinking with your new ability to manage your emotions and keep your emotions from controlling your life. Change how you see, and you will find a new world.

Benefits of Positive Self-talk

"If you don't like something, change it. If you can't change it, change the way that you think about it."

—Mary Engelbreit

Yoga believes the words we think or say out loud produce a physical vibration. Repetition of these words and the physical vibration changes how we view of the world.

Repeating choice words helps direct your mind away from negative thoughts and focus on a positive life. The Sanskrit *mantra* means "instrument for thinking." The method is to repeat mantras when you relax or meditate or whenever you can fit them into your schedule.

Benefits of Positive Thinking
- Achieved goals
- Improvement in athleticism
- Higher coping skills
- Better organized thoughts
- Improved physical and psychological wellbeing
- Greater resistance to the common cold
- Happier working hours
- Healthier overall
- Improved recovery
- Increased confidence
- Less anxiety and depression
- Longer life span
- More job offers and promotions
- Reduction in anger and stress

13 SELF-TALK: MOVING FROM NEGATIVE TO POSITIVE

"I hear, and I forget. I see, and I remember. I do, and I understand."

—*Confucius*

In this two-part exercise, you will learn about positive self-talk. You will then identify a negative self-talk and convert it into a positive self-talk.

Exercise C: Mantras for Calming Anxiety

1. Practice saying mantras out loud.

    a. "I am capable."

    b. "I know who I am, and I am enough."

    c. "I will be present in all that I do."

    d. "I choose to think thoughts that serve me well."

    e. "I will reach for a better feeling."

    f. "I share my happiness with those around me."

    g. "My body is my vehicle in life. I will fill it with goodness."

    h. "I feel energetic and alive."

    i. "My life is unfolding beautifully."

    j. "I am confident."

    k. "I always observe before reacting."

    l. "I know that with time and effort, I can achieve."

    m. "I love challenges and the things I learn by overcoming them."

    n. "Each step on my path is taking me closer to where I want to be."

2. Practice speaking to yourself in the first person: "I am capable" and in the third person: "Michelle is capable."

Exercise D: Identify and Change Negative Self-talk

Identify a negative thought or phrase, then turn it into a positive one. It should reflect the person you want to become and the life you want to live.

	Identify a negative thought or phrase.	Turn your negative thought or phrase into a positive one.
Example 1	I never finish what I start.	I will set aside time to achieve my goals.
Example 2	I look terrible and feel anxious.	I will sleep and shower.
Example 3	I have to go to work.	I want to go to work.
My Statement 1		
My Statement 2		
My Statement 3		

14 HABITS

"We have met the enemy, and he is us."

—Walt Kelly

The above phrase first appeared on an Earth Day poster in 1970. Its creator, Walt Kelly, is also the creator of the *Pogo* comic strip, which later boasted use of this wise quote.

Undoubtedly, bad habits waste our energy. Yoga calls this our prana, our life force. Bad habits keep you from accomplishing goals and fully living our life. They can have a negative effect on your physical and mental health. We all struggle to find freedom from bad habits, but those who break them tend to replace them with other habits. The key is to shift your old habits to new, better ones. It is easier to make these changes if you focus on the benefit rather than simply pointing out faults that require correction. To do this, we will practice two effective strategies for habit shifting, and it will work, regardless of what habit you are trying to change.

The first is learning to unlearn. The world is ever changing, and to survive, you must be willing to change as well. To succeed in life, you must continue to learn, unlearn, and relearn. This is why we spend many years in school. Rather than trying to learn how to overcome your existing bad habits, try to focus on unlearning it by shifting it to a new, positive habit.

Before you can unlearn a habit, you should first understand the root cause. Bad habits can be a way of dealing with stress or boredom. Habits like biting your nails, overspending, drinking, or wasting time on the internet are often responses to stress and boredom. These are sometimes surface issues, with something deeper lying beneath them. Working with these issues can be difficult and uncomfortable, but if you are serious about making changes, you must push past the discomfort and change your habits and misbeliefs.

Remember that you rarely remove a habit. You only shift your old habit to a new one. Thinking about habits this way will help you to shift out of bad habits. Perhaps, instead of telling yourself, "I need to stop biting my nails," try, "When I get stressed, I will practice a breathing exercise".

The second strategy is to keep from giving up too early. Unlearning and relearning takes extra time and work. This will force you to change parts of your life and also the people you surround yourself with. Studies have shown that to create or shift a habit, you must practice a behavior for twenty-eight to forty days. After that, it should be much easier. Have you noticed that many diets claim to be thirty-day miracle cures, and fitness studios offer low-priced thirty-day trials? There is good reason for that, because they are hoping you will form a habit that will keep you coming back for more.

Remember that failing is how we learn. Be mindful that change is difficult and look for ways to remain accountable. Cut out as many triggers as possible. If you smoke when you drink, stay out of bars. If you have a sweet tooth, do not buy treats for the house. Shifting a habit is much easier if you can avoid the things that cause them. Change your environment to make it easier to shift bad habits and create new, healthy ones. Breaking bad habits takes time and effort, but persistence is the most important part. Most people who shift bad habits fail multiple times before they succeed. If you do not have immediate success, stay patient, and you will see positive results.

Benefits of Positive Habits

"We are what we repeatedly do. Excellence, then, is not an act but a habit."

—Aristotle

A *habit* is a behavior pattern we follow until it becomes almost involuntary. A *positive habit* is a positive action or behavior.

Benefits of Positive Habits
- Better choices
- Boosts energy
- Combats diseases
- Controls weight
- Enhances outcomes
- Happier relationships
- Healthful lifestyle
- Helps you reach your goals
- Higher spiritual connection
- Improves longevity
- Improves mood
- Increases competence
- More energy
- Function more efficiently
- Promotes comfort
- Saves time
- Sharpens focus
- Steadfast confidence
- Stronger foundation for life

15 HABIT SHIFTING

In this two-part exercise, you will identify good and bad habit specifics and decide upon a habit that you wish to change. Then you will learn steps to create a new habit. The habits do not need to be similar. Remember that failure is part of the learning process.

Exercise E: Shift a Bad Habit, Part 1

1 Identify three benefits you will receive from calming your anxiety.	
Example 1	• A happier life
Example 2	• Less physical pain
Example 3	• Find more meaning
My Plan 1	
My Plan 2	
My Plan 3	

2	Identify a habit you want to change.	Identify a habit you want to create.
Example A	• I bite my nails.	• Practice a breathing exercise to calm my anxiety.
Example B	• I bite my nails.	• Quietly and slowly count to ten to calm my anxiety.
My Plan		

3	How often does your habit occur?	How often do you want to participate in your new habit or replace the urge to participate in an old one?
Example A	• 2-3 times a day	• Create a new habit.
Example B	• 5-6 times a day	• Replace the urge to do my old habit.
My plan		

4	Where are you when your habit occurs?	Identify ways to avoid triggers to your anxiety.
Example A	• I am at work, in a meeting with my boss.	• I can practice a subtle breathing exercise during the meeting.
Example B	• I am at work or at home, worried about having to give a presentation.	• I can practice a breathing exercise at home or work when I become anxious.
My Plan		

5	Who are you with when your habit occurs?	Identify ways to avoid people who increase your anxiety.
Example A	• I am with my boss, in a meeting.	• I cannot avoid my boss. I can stay mindful during meetings.
Example B	• I am by myself, worrying about giving a presentation.	• I can slowly count to ten.
My Plan		

6	What triggers the behavior?	How can you avoid the triggers to your anxiety?
Example A	• Thinking about being asked a hard question during a meeting at work.	• I cannot avoid work or meetings. I can prepare answers to questions my boss has asked in the past. • I can prepare answers to questions I would ask if I were my boss.
Example B	• I become anxious before I have to give a presentation.	• I cannot avoid giving presentations. I can practice in front of a mirror or a friend to be better prepared. • I can prepare answers to questions I think people will ask.
My Plan		

7	What has prevented you from shifting your habit?	What may keep you from making this habit shift permanent?
Example A	• I do not stay mindful about shifting my habit when I become anxious.	• I can place frequent reminders in front of me for when I become anxious.
Example B	• I forget about trying to change my habit after a day or two.	• I can place reminders in front of me so I do not stop trying too soon.
My Plan		

8	What inspired you to make this change?	What can inspire you to make this habit shift work long term?
Example A	• I feel horrible all the time.	• A picture of me smiling and having a good time
Example B	• I ruined an important relationship because I was so unpleasant.	• A picture of me or someone else who appears overwhelmed by anxiety
My Plan		

9	What old habit are you shifting to a new habit?	Identify other strategies you can use to reinforce your habit shift.
Example A	• I bite my nails.	• I can paint my nails or rub vinegar on them so they taste bad when I try to bite them.
Example B	• I bite my nails.	• I can keep the three benefits I will get from calming my anxiety in my top desk drawer and write them on my bathroom mirror.
My Plan A		
My Plan B		
My Plan C		
My Plan D		

Exercise F: Shift a Bad Habit, Part 2

1 Identify three benefits you will receive from calming your anxiety.	
Example 1	• I want to enjoy work rather than dreading it.
Example 2	• I want to feel happy.
Example 3	• I want stronger friendships and better relationships with my family.
My Plan 1	
My Plan 2	
My Plan 3	

2	Identify a habit you want to change.	Identify a habit you want to create.
Example A	• I do not exercise, and I feel terrible most of the time.	• I want to exercise more often.
Example B	• I watch a lot of television after work, which increases my anxiety.	• I want to spend more time with friends and family.
My Plan		

3	How often does your habit occur?	How often do you want to participate in your new habit or replace your urge to participate in your old one?
Example A	• I watch television every day after work.	• I want to practice yoga or exercise three times a week.
Example B	• I watch television every day after work.	• I want to spend time with friends and family three times a week.
My plan		

4	Where are you when your habit occurs?	Identify ways to avoid triggers to your old habit.
Example A	• I am at home, watching television.	• I can find a friend to go to yoga class or the gym with me and keep me accountable.
Example B	• I am at home, watching television.	• I can schedule time to visit with friends and family to keep me from reverting to my old habit.
My Plan		

5	Who are you with when your habit occurs?	Identify ways to avoid the person you are with or better manage the situation.
Example A	• I am by myself, watching television.	• Before leaving work, I can schedule something to do at home other than watching television.
Example B	• I am by myself, watching television.	• After work, I can run errands instead of going home to watch television.
My Plan		

6	What triggers cause the behavior?	How can you avoid the triggers to your old habit?
Example A	• I am tired when I leave work.	• I can arrange to meet a friend at yoga class or the gym and go there directly from work.
Example B	• I lack motivation when I leave work.	• I can arrange to meet friends or family after work without first going home.
My Plan		

7	What has prevented you from shifting your habit?	What can help you make this habit shift permanent?
Example A	• I lack time and energy after work to exercise	• I can put a note on my dashboard to remind me of the benefits I will get from yoga and working out.
Example B	• I do not stay mindful about spending time with friends and family.	• I can place reminders in front of me so I do not forget.
My Plan		

8	What inspired you to make this change?	What will inspire you to make this habit shift work in the long term?
Example A	• I want to feel better about my appearance and enjoy the health benefits.	• A picture of me smiling while practicing yoga or exercising at the gym.
Example B	• I feel anxious and depressed most of the time.	• I can create a vision board to remind myself of what inspires me to spend more time with friends and family.
My Plan		

9	Positive Habit You Plan to Create	Other Strategies to Reinforce Your Habit Shift
Example A	• I want to exercise three times a week.	• I can sign up for yoga and exercise newsletters or podcasts to remind myself of the benefits of working out.
Example B	• I want to spend time with friends and family three times a week.	• I can write down the three benefits I will get from exercising and spending more time with friends and family and keep it in my top desk drawer as a reminder. •
My Plan A		
My Plan B		
My Plan C		

PERSONAL SUMMARY

Question	Your Response
1 Which parts were most meaningful?	
2 Which parts were least meaningful?	
3 Which exercise(s) do you think will work best for creating change in your life?	
4 Do you plan to share any of the strategies and exercises with others? If so, which ones and with whom?	
5 Did you discover an area, habit, or belief that you would like to change in your life?	

ABOUT THE AUTHOR

Ken Heptig is an author who trains yoga teachers how to add yoga philosophy to their classes to improve the lives of their students. His first book, *Yoga Secrets: 52 Life-Changing Secrets,* published in 2016, is among the first books to be written with focus on teaching yoga philosophy during any style of yoga practice. Ken created a method to make yoga philosophy easy for teachers and students, following "The Eight Limbs of Yoga" concept from *The Yoga Sutras of Patanjali.* He is the founder of the GoalYoga™ Yoga Teacher Training School.

Ken's practice of yoga spans two decades, and he believes that to fill your life with joy, your yoga classes must include fun and humor. For this reason, every class he teaches is fraught with life-changing lessons, fun, and silly jokes.

In early childhood, Ken asked questions that others thought were just odd. When he started his yoga practice, he asked many more questions, demanding to know the true meaning of the words and phrases he heard in class. Years later, as a yoga teacher himself, Ken felt a strong desire to explain these placebo phrases to his students, but he found this to be a far more difficult feat than he expected. This led him to begin uncovering *Yoga Secrets* for himself and others.

At that point, Ken changed his career focus from things to people. He was managing and growing a national technology company at the time, one he co-founded thirty years earlier, but he taught yoga and created lessons as often as he could.

While he taught his students to ask better questions, he had to ask one of himself: "What should I do next?" The answer was easy, but it demanded a difficult transformation in his life. His passion was to share his fun and easy method of transforming people's lives. He realized that knowing what you want to do and actually doing it are very different, and his peers would not understand or approve of the change. It took time for Ken to realize he was not in search of the tribe's approval. What he sought was his true self, so he had to make the change.

Ken had adopted the beliefs of others that yoga was not a career, that it was merely something meant for exercise and fun. He had to unlearn this belief and relearn a new one, which he found very challenging. Ironically, he found help in the very lessons he was using to create life changes in his students.

Since then, Ken Heptig has tested and refined his method and lessons through thousands of yoga classes. This simple method uses specific techniques to create lasting change. Several of the techniques include persistence, clarity, learning to unlearn, and frequency versus duration.

Ken's *Yoga Secrets* series informs yoga teachers, students, and others of life-changing lessons that result in positive life changes. He knows from experience that yoga results in better balance, focus, discipline, and strength, but he hopes all will aim for more, for the miraculous lives they deserve and can achieve.

Ken always lived with a fear of writing. While he could compose boring, polite business communication, he experienced anxiety when attempting to write anything else. As he penned *Yoga Secrets,* he lived in a constant state of fear that he would not accomplish that goal, but his motivation was the pain of knowing that not sharing the lessons would be much greater than the pain of writing the book. He used the lessons in *Yoga Secrets* to overcome his anxiety of writing.

He has a background in fitness and health. Before yoga, Ken taught aerobic classes, ran marathons, and backpacked. He holds a bachelor of science in food science and nutrition from NCSU and an MBA in information systems from Golden Gate University.

Made in the USA
Middletown, DE
03 May 2021